THE DEVIL
WAS AN ANGEL, TOO

Autobiography of

Anthony Eagle, Jr.

DEDICATION

I want to thank my mom for showing me what to be
and how to care and love the people in my life.

My kids for giving me a reason to turn my life around and
work on being the best dad possible.

And I thank God for showing me His grace.

CONTENTS

Acknowledgments   Pg # 1

1   Introduction   Pg # 3

2   Early Years   Pg # 9

3   Fight or Flight   Pg # 17

4   Grandma/handtalk   Pg # 25

5   Devil Without a Cause   Pg # 31

6   Family Above All   Pg # 43

7   United States Penitentiary   Pg # 55

8   Good Wolf, Bad Wolf   Pg # 61

9   Social Media Fame   Pg # 75

10   Wear It Like Armour   Pg # 79

ACKNOWLEDGMENTS

To Mom, Dad, Kat, and Angela for helping me
make all of this happen.

To my supporters for always encouraging
me to keep going.

ANTHONY EAGLE, JR.

1 INTRODUCTION

Our most basic emotional need is not to fall in love, but to be genuinely loved by another, to know a love that grows out of reason and choice, not instinct.

-Gary Chapman (The 5 Love Languages)

ANTHONY EAGLE, JR.

I'm not here to brag about my story. I don't wish for anyone to go through what I had to go through. But my story must be told, even if it only helps one person to realize that the path they're going down needs to be changed for the better. Or, perhaps you just need a bit of hope as you watch your own child go down a road of wrong choices- I'm here to encourage you and tell you to never give up.

I'm also not telling this story because I want something. And I definitely don't want you to think, oh here's another person telling his prison story because, let's be honest, prison was the worst thing that happened to me in every sense of the word. It was the worst thing I could've done to my kids, to the victims I created behind it, to the people I hurt in the process, and the most extreme feeling of being alone that you could possibly imagine. I lost loved ones when I was locked up because I was "cool" at one point, because I can throw down. Look, there's not anything cool about my story, but what would be cool is if you could learn from it.

I've had a hard life, and it wasn't because I grew up in a home that was neglectful or anything like that. I'm a master of self- sabotage. If there's a way to mess up a good thing, I'm going to be the one that finds it. Now, with that said, I do want you to know that this isn't going to be an easy story to read. I've had bad things happen to me, and I've also done some bad things, but the experiences are what led me to be the person I am today.

Sometimes, we have to go through the pain of being broken before we can be made whole again. It's not always going to be easy, but if you can just find the strength to persevere, it will be worth it!

I hope you find inspiration in my story. Maybe you can find some parts of it to relate to. If I can make it through this and still come out seeing the light, then I know you can, too. I want this book to help someone. There are so many people out there hurting, hopeless, looking for a reason to wake up and find joy again. I want you to know that you are worth it! You are here for a reason. Please don't give up. Your life is worth saving.

ANTHONY EAGLE, JR.

2 EARLY YEARS

I looked up.
High above us, the stars were becoming shapes,
as the clouds had done that afternoon. First there was a coyote, then
a bear, hawk, and many other creatures, both animal and human.
Chanting, the Star People encircled us. "They are the spirits of the
Old Ones who once walked on this earth."

The Star People- a Lakota Story by S.D. Nelson

I grew up on an Ojibwe Native American reservation in Michigan. Being on the rez is another form of control. I do appreciate the land and housing, but it does put people in a bind. They don't learn independence, and instead rely on the government to provide for them. The conditions are very poor, and addiction runs rampant, setting up the supply and demand for drugs, alcohol, and crime. With that being said, I loved being around my Native culture, it's my identity and what I will pass on to my children. As a kid, I loved to sing, dance, and play drums. The powwows brought us all close and made me feel at one with the Creator.

So many traditions have been lost. Natives would pass down history and stories through spoken word and dance. For so long, they were forbidden by the government to have powwows, dance in tribal outfits, or express their beliefs. As a kid, I would sing, dance and drum in honor of my heritage. I hope to bring some awareness and appreciation to our culture through this book.

My mom raised five kids on her own. My dad was in prison until I was eleven, so it was up to her to be all things to us. She had a lot to deal with, and some of her choices might not have been perfect, but we never questioned her love for us. I advocate for women because as a Native American man, really just as a *man*, that's what you should do. But I support women because I was raised by a single mother, and to me she is literally a superhero!

Single mothers have my highest respect. Her priority is her children. If she chooses to give her time to a man, he needs to respect that and understand that she is worth everything because her time is precious. God put us here to support each other, and what would I look like if a woman was trying to reach goals, or feel special, or wanted me to notice her, but I wouldn't acknowledge her worth? All people hold value. If you don't like her point of view, you can walk away, but you still need to respect her.

Mom was the glue that held us together. She was our consistency, our normalcy, the one person we could always rely on. Every night she made sure she was there to sing to us as we went to sleep. As a kid, I didn't always appreciate that, but now that I'm older I see how special those moments were

I am the second of five children, and although I wasn't the oldest, I did play a role as the man of the house quite a bit. I would often be in charge of looking after my brothers and sisters while my mom was at work. My oldest brother was a horrible asthmatic, he and I

played a lot of video games together since his activity had to be limited. I loved being physically active and playing sports, but I didn't want him to feel left out.

We spent a lot of time waiting in the ER or sitting in the hospital when he was having a bad attack. If mom didn't have a sitter, I would watch my sisters while she tended to Joshua and my baby brother. I had to make sure Joshua had his medicine available and watch for the signs of a life-threatening attack, which ultimately ended up in me saving his life. I visited him every day while he was in the ICU. No one was going to keep me away from my brother. So, at a young age, I held the responsibility of making sure everyone was taken care of. Even today, I feel responsible for my family and their well-being.

I was always kind, respectful, loved to cuddle and show affection. My dad didn't like that I was a "Mama's boy". I was always very loving unless my dad was around and then I would pull away and

put on the tough act. Mom kept his visitation with us tied up in courts while my dad continued to go in and out of prison. I longed for a relationship with him, and when he was out of prison I'd sit and wait for him to pick me up, but was more often disappointed and left feeling abandoned when he never showed.

I had many men in my life to help me when my dad wasn't there. Mom knew we needed a man as a role model, and her dad, Grandpa Pete, often filled that gap. Although my mom was not a regular church goer at that time, she would have our grandpa pick us up and drop us off at church.

To be honest, Grandpa Pete hated everyone but the girls, and could be mean, but he showed me how to do manly things- like how to work on houses, paint, and fix cars. He didn't tell me he loved me

until I was 21. He hated the fact that I looked like my dad, but towards the end he realized he'd messed up. I guess we're all like that. At the end of life, we let everybody know we love them. He became a really good person later on, but like most of us, his childhood affected the way he treated us. I still miss him to this day.

I was a very adventurous kid! I've always loved exploring the woods, fishing, camping, you name it. My Uncle Mike tried to teach me the right things in life. He was a good man. Unfortunately, at that time I wasn't interested in the right things. I wanted excitement and the excitement of seeing what I could get away with.

My Uncle Jamie filled my need for thrill seeking! When I was sixteen, I was with him in Nashville. We went to Denim and Diamonds and I was talking to my uncle about girls and he's like have you ever been with a black girl?

So, the next day we went to the club, and I followed Uncle Jamie to a big group of black girls. He left with one of the girls to the dance floor and just left me with them. This one girl smiles at me with a gold tooth and we danced to Nellie and Kellie- Dilemmas- we eventually ended up in a bad part of town at their house. It was a fun night, but we got out of there fast!

Another time, we had a dude- our weed guy- named Raymond. He had about ten pit bulls and grew pot in his backyard. Nashville has a brick wall that's used for dispensing. So, we decided we were going to rob him. The whole month before, I'm playing with the pit bulls. So, they knew me, and as I'm playing with the dogs my uncle cut down this guy's plants and we hung them in my little trailer. The guy came to the door with a gun, and I answered the door with a bat. My uncle Jamie hit him in the head with a rock and the rest is history…

Aside from not having my dad around, school was one of many obstacles that I faced. I have learning issues, ADD and dyslexia. I was placed in Special Education classes because of this. I was pretty good at math, but anything that required reading was difficult for me. I hated that so many kids in my classes were bullied, and I took it upon myself to protect them. Even to this day, I can't stand a bully.

In fact, one of the reasons I started learning sign language in depth is from an incident that happened at a pizza place. I saw a deaf guy lose one of his earpieces and people were bullying him. So, I got pissed off and started signing to him to help. After that, I was determined to learn more.

You have a minimum amount of time to make an impact in this world. I look at life different because of the struggles I faced. We each have our own struggles, and we have our own monsters. How you choose to let that out – see that's your choice. You can choose to be toxic or volatile, or you can choose to be loving, caring, and understanding in all situations. That also includes understanding your enemy. It's going to be a challenge, and definitely not what you want to do, but if we could just approach life from a level of understanding there would be much more peace in this world.

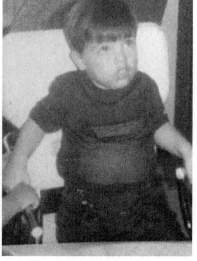

3 FIGHT OR FLIGHT

When all you know is fight or flight, red flags and
Butterflies all feel the same.

-Cindy Cherie

ANTHONY EAGLE, JR.

I was a happy kid, carefree, lovable, and my mom taught me to turn the other cheek and walk away from trouble. Because my dad was in prison until I was eleven, I learned how to be a man from listening to rap music. I had a very distorted view of what it meant to "be a man".

I was young and thought I had to live that life to be part of it. My mom was raising us kids the best she could, but I constantly searched for other influences, mainly bad ones. I started smoking pot around fourteen years old, and my mom got overwhelmed and fed up with my rebellious  behavior. When my dad was released from another prison term, my mom let me go live with him because I kept getting into trouble and she hoped that he would be able to straighten me out.

Unfortunately, it was quite the opposite. You see, my dad had decided that he wanted a gangster as a son, so that's exactly what I became. He indoctrinated me easily because as a kid all I wanted was approval from him. I became whatever he told me to be because I loved him, and he was the man of the family- the hero in my eyes.

My life took a completely different route one day at the park where me and my brother and sisters were playing. My older brother got into an altercation with a kid, and me and the other kid got into it, and I tackled him and held my fist up to punch him. Right before I hit him, I heard my mom's voice say *the bigger person walks away*. So, instead of fighting, I decided to just leave and head home because, up to that point, I had been taught to turn the other cheek. When we got home, Josh started bragging about what had happened, and I felt good, like it was one of the best moments I had ever had.

My dad heard about it and didn't say a word, so he put us all in the car and drove to the store to get us chips and a pop. Well, he didn't get me anything, so I'm still thinking oh man, I'm going to get the best prize, and I was still so proud of myself. So, we head back home, and he's still not really talking to me, other than trying to get the story out of me. So, I told him, and when we got home he headed inside right away. When I got inside, he hollered for me, and I went down to the basement where he was. The moment I walked down there, he hit me across the face with a rod from a tent, blood was everywhere, and he drug me straight to the park and ordered me to beat up the kid, to handle it. So that's what I did, I fought the kid, and he told me if I ever skipped out on a fight again that's what would happen to me.

We all have this instinct to either stand our ground and defend ourselves or run as fast as we can to escape. My father robbed me of my fight or flight. I was only given one option- to fight, and I better not lose or else I would face the consequences when I got home. The mental havoc this put on me was suffocating. I had to push away the primal instinct to run away and push my fears away.

Another time, while I was staying with my dad, he decided that I needed to "become a man." I didn't know what he meant by that. He walked me to his bedroom, and I saw my stepmom lying naked on the bed. My dad told me to go hit that, and that's how I lost my virginity. It never happened again. It felt good to me, I had my dad's approval, but she turned mean, and I feel like it's because she thought I had violated her. After that, I became reckless when it came to sex, but in my mind, I was "being a man."

I wish I could say that life with my dad became easier. It didn't.... I started smoking pot because of my family's influence. I became so "cool" that I started dealing drugs. The gangster life was what I lived for and would ultimately be my downfall. I started using harder drugs and tried crack in Florida with a friend.

Between the ages of twelve and fourteen I rebelled hard and was placed in foster care because of my behavior. This mom and her son were horrible to me, so I beat up her son and got sent to a group home in Minnesota. I got in fights there and got sent to a boot camp In Michigan. I conned the system until I did what I had to do to get out.

Then, I went back home to my mom, acted even crazier, and started hanging out with older kids.

Because my dad was in and out of prison so much, I didn't learn how to be a man, how to be a dad, or how to raise a family. He wasn't around when we needed him, and it was hard on my siblings and my mom. No matter what your parents put you through, there is always this longing to be with family. I still had a deep ache to belong, to be accepted, to gain the love and approval from my dad.

This is where trying to understand comes in. People can change. I NEED for you to understand this. My dad was not a terrible person. He had the kindest heart of anyone I knew. He just grew up  different and thought he was doing right by teaching us not to back down, by making us tough. I did what he said because I was constantly seeking his approval. But through everything, we never once doubted our father's love for us.

Unfortunately, my dad got his life straightened out after it was too late. I was already strung out and in prison when he started getting his life together. For me, though, I was hopeless and scared, wondering if I would ever get out of this hell I was living.

My dad's mission was to help those caught up in the legal system, to help those reentering life after being in prison, and to make a difference in the justice system.

Sadly, he was killed on August 3, 2012, in a motorcycle accident.

I was able to publish the book that he had written. He never had a chance to do that while he was alive. I decided to write my book as a continuance to his, and hope that one day my sister can write her story as the final chapter.

ANTHONY EAGLE, JR.

4 NOKOMIS

(MY GRANDMOTHER- OJIBWE)

ANTHONY EAGLE, JR.

My grandmother is an amazing woman. She is my hero. I looked up to her and learned so much from her as a kid. She made sure that us kids knew who we were, what it meant to be Native, passed down stories and traditions, and instilled pride in us for our tribe.

One day, she gave me an eagle feather and told me that it was meant for me to have. She then proceeded to tell me that when you put your intentions into the universe, no matter what you believe, it has to connect to the Creator. Well, Native Americans believe that the Magizii, the eagle, can fly high enough to bring our messages to the Creator, to bring our intentions to light.

The bottom of the feather represents my life.
At the beginning my life was easy, everything was handed to me. As I became a man, I understood life was going to hand me the cards I didn't want, but I needed to hear them and ended up broken and frayed. My path becomes narrow, but at the end it is full of love.

My grandmother is the reason I know hand talk. She would teach me how to sign and told me stories of our ancestors. I take pride in the fact that my grandma took the time to teach me this valuable tradition of our culture. I take pride in being able to share this with the world

Hand talk was used for over 200 years by neighboring tribes to communicate with one another. It was the first language for deaf Natives. By the late 1800's, tens of thousands of Native Americans used it. That all changed when the federal government instituted a policy designed to "civilize" tribal people. Today, there may be just a few dozen users.

I didn't start posting videos with hand talk to cause any kind of negativity. However, the ASL community came at me hard. The actual culture, at least in America, is that sign language was the first language for Native Americans and white settlers to be able to correspond and talk. The language barrier wasn't as great if they had sign language to use. Later, the settlers used their knowledge of hand talk to form what we now know as ASL.

My grandmother told me many stories as a child, and every time she talked, she was always using her hands. Language is a culture. Hand talk is part of my culture, and now I also incorporate SEE-signing exact English. I will forever be grateful to my grandma, because without her there is no me. My grandmother is a very special person, and her light will live on through me and our family.

I come from royalty.
This is Chief Joseph Whetung

Grandmother in
tribal dress.

Never forget where you come from.

5 DEVIL WITHOUT A CAUSE

Poison is anything that exceeds our needs.

ANTHONY EAGLE, JR.

It always felt like something was missing from my life. Me and my buddy Don would use alcohol and drugs to cover up whatever pain we had inside of us. Don and I had a lot of common hurts and experiences. We didn't want to deal with any of it, so we went down a dark road for many years.

I asked Don to contribute to this part of my story. Here is what he wanted to share with you:

At this time in our lives, we were lost, missing, searching for something. We used alcohol and other substances to mask whatever path or problems we were trying to support.

I was raised by an alcoholic mother and watched through a keyhole as she got tied to a chair and beat up while I was locked in my bedroom. I was always locked in my room. Over the years, I was subjected to horrendous forms of abuse until I finally told someone what was happening. I thank God that my grandma took me and adopted me. So, you see, Tony and I have gone through a lot as kids, and that was a common bond as we grew older.

Tony was still a good human even before prison.

One time, there was a party on the rez at a house that we partied at a lot. Gerald's was the party house. So mid  party I met this girl Jaime, and we headed downstairs to a bedroom. After a bit, I walked back up the stairs and as soon as my foot hit the top stair, I hear the front door get booted in. I look and see this guy, Mike, that we all know, he's a sketchy human. Well Mike and his ex were going through a breakup, and I remember seeing her with some guy before I went downstairs, so I'm thinking someone is fixing to get the shit beat out of them. I turn my head and somehow his ex is now next to ME! Before I even know what's happened, I'm being punched and hit the floor. Next thing I see is Tony set his beer down calmly and walk over to Mike and slam him back and forth off the ground kinda' like a cartoon. He's yelling the whole time- why the fuck did you hit him?!?! Tony mopped the floor with him. That's the kind of friend he was. He would let a little go, but he saw the sucker punch, knew it was fucked up and handled it right there.

Another night in Marquette, Tony decided he wanted to go to the club, so we all get ready and head out. We aren't even at this place for fifteen minutes, and one of the bouncers said something slick aimed at Tony. I think it was a negative comment towards Natives. Next thing I know, Tony fires at one of them and immediately put the dude to sleep. So now I'm like  Okay here we go, and right then a big ass bouncer comes up from behind Tony and bear hugs him. Tony grabs his thumb and I'm pretty sure he broke it because the guy let him go and grabbed his hand and backed up. After that, we had one more in front of him.

Tony and this guy are both big people, so they both start firing and connecting hard. This bouncer had gauged ears and, next thing I see, is Tony grabbing the gauged earring and ripping it out of this guy's ear. His ear was super fucked up and I guarantee needed stitches, so we figured that was our time to leave. So, we continue our party back at the apartment, and about five minutes later I hear a laugh and see Tony with this evil smile as he tosses the earring across the table. So, I hear this *ting ting ting* as this bloody thing hits the table and I hear Tony saying "Well I got him!! HA HA!" Tony is a different breed. I've never seen him with my eyes lose a fight.

Tony was such a good dude that he had a couple spots in Esky that I could crash if I didn't have anywhere to go. I was in a bad place for a few years after my divorce and losing my daughter, that I just gave up on life.

Tony always seemed to help me out with money, or with a job. Even through his violence he had a huge heart. Tony always had some sort of hustle and motivation. Where he usually had money, I was so caught up in my addictions and battling mental illness without meds that I was broke and directionless. He always took me in and expected nothing in return.

The last interaction between Tony and I before he went to prison, we were at the Stardust with a bunch of Natives. I knew something was wrong because we were not talking. Next thing I know, he picks me up by the throat right off my feet, and slammed me against this huge window. Thank God it didn't break. He still had enough love for me to not swing and he let me walk away. He could have hurt me bad and chose not to. That's the last time we spoke until after prison. He called me and apologized, and we didn't miss a beat. We will always be best friends; he's saved me more times than I can count. *end of Don's letter*

Don and I didn't get back together until about ten years later after I went to prison a couple times and I saw that his brother died in prison. There are people placed in your life for certain periods, and then they're gone.   Me and Don will always have that bond. No matter what is going on, or how long it's been, we will always pick right back up where we left off.

The day my life changed...

You don't look at selling drugs as hurting anyone, it's just providing something that someone wants. Supply and Demand. It helped me get money for my family. You don't realize you're hurting others or their families.

My own children were hurt because I was taken away to do time. The unfortunate reality is that no one grows up the same, and I viewed a man as someone who could fight their ass off, and I definitely wasn't going to cry or let anyone see me as weak. In my mind, I was untouchable.

If you look up my name, you'll find many versions of why I ended up in prison. The truth is I was saving my sister. I had surprised my sisters and met them at the local casino/bar. When I got there this certain person was also at the casino, and he refused to take the hint when my sister told him to stop touching her. When I saw him, we looked at each other and I just gave a signal that meant "enough". He looked at me and I thought it was over.

I left to go see my cousin. I called my sisters to see how they were doing. So, we decide to meet up again at the Q Master Bar. I get a Bud Lite and hear a commotion. That guy was at the bar, and he decided to put his hands on my sister again, and she kicked him. He landed on his ass, and I told her to go upstairs to her apartment. They kicked the guy out, but about five minutes later I just didn't feel easy, so I go to check on my sister and that's when I stopped this guy from assaulting her. I beat his ass. I drug him down the stairs, and I beat his ass some more. Truth be told, I thought he was gone, and I stopped. I never wanted to hurt anyone that bad, but I didn't understand what the fuck he was doing. The next day, I was arrested.

I'm not going to tell you that my actions were right. What I am going to tell you is that I would defend anyone who was being assaulted like that. I will never stand back and allow that to happen. We have to protect the innocent- women, children, and the elderly. Did I go too far? Possibly. Would I do it over again if it meant saving my sister? Absolutely...

As a young man, a lot of things go through your mind when you realize you are about to go to prison for many years. At that time, prison time was just another badge of honor, another opportunity to prove that I was a gangster and a badass.

I had a reporter ask me how I felt about the sentencing and my reply was, "it is what it is."

My mom and family stepped in and took care of the boys (I had sole custody). Every once in a while, their mom's sister would take the boys and spend time with them. My kids were always taken care of, and for that I will be forever grateful.

ANTHONY EAGLE, JR.

6 UNITED STATES PENITENTIARY

The definition of insanity is doing the same thing over and over again and expecting a different result.

-Einstein

ANTHONY EAGLE, JR.

MDOC Number: **508451**

SID Number: **2172545P**

Name: **ANTHONY LEONARD EAGLE JR.**

Racial Identification: **Native American**

Gender: **Male**

Hair: **Brown**

Eyes: **Hazel**

Height: **6' 0"**

Weight: **245 lbs.**

The United States Federal Prison System is a hard place. It's a very dangerous place, as well. I'm not going to try to tell it's not. Prison was the worst obstacle that I've ever had to get through. I had to survive. I had to come home. There were no choices. And, when you get to a place where demons are real, where I tell you face to face you look into another man's eyes and they're not a man, they are something else because they will snatch your life like it doesn't matter. Humanity doesn't exist at that level.

I can tell you Hell exists on earth because not only will you get a physical beat down in a place like that, but you will also be emotionally scarred for the rest of your life. The harsh reality is that you will never be the same. Every person that walks into your life, you're going to wonder about them and their intentions. They will never get the benefit of the doubt because they have to *show* you. You're going to notice small things, and relationships will have problems because the way you think and the way they think will not match up.

When you first enter the prison system, they get you on a plane right away. No holds barred, they get you on *Con-Air* and they fly you to Oklahoma City. Once there, you go into this big room, and you don't know what is happening. This is where they tell you where you're going, they're going to do all of your physical stuff, they see if you're healthy, if you got HIV, and other things of that nature. So, you get done and you get to this line, and at the very end they tell you where you're going to go. I was not at all excited about this process anyway, but to top it off they told me I was going to the Hazelton United States Penitentiary in West Virginia, on the top of a mountain!

I'll never forget that day. I walked into that prison in the same scenario as Oklahoma City, you go through the same process, you'll talk to the prison police and they'll ask you who you run with, and you're gonna run with somebody because that's just how it goes in federal prison, it doesn't mean you're weak or nothing like that, it's just how that prison system is ran. It's ran in groups. When you get there, they ask who you run with and divide you up according to your race. I realized later in life that this fulfills a much larger agenda than anyone is even aware of.

So, we finally get done there, and it's late and we are getting down to the dorm and walking through the prison, and I can't help but think that this place is HUGE! It seems like the corridor goes on for miles. And as you get to the dorm you think all eyes are on you but really, they're just looking at you out of curiosity and they look to see if any of the new guys are their race. They told me my room was upstairs, and ya' know, I didn't even know gang bangin' existed on this level, but my roommate comes walking towards me, his name was E and he did most of my tats.

E was tattooed from his face to his back, just all over tatted. So, he comes walking up to me and is asking if I'm his bunky. So, I'm like yea and he's like nice to meet you- you want a soda or something? I'm like NO man, I ain't taking nothing from nobody, I'm on my own two feet!! E turned out to be a really good dude, but I was woke up that  night, my very first night, and E was sharpening a knife. The sad reality is, as you walk into prison, you will be offered a knife. That was me being offered a knife. I can't say much about that knife or what happened to it, but it was about as big as the back of my arm.

I had this homeboy, we used to call him Duck, we called him duck for a reason, and he thought every single female wanted him. So, one day he came to the cell, and he said hey you know that girl down in Psychology she's into me, well I got an appointment today and she's been wanting me to come in there so I'm going to go in there and see her. I said Duck stop playing, that psychologist don't want you! But he insisted that she did, and when he came back from the meeting, he was bubbly as hell and he kept going on about how she wanted him. I asked him why he thought that, and he said he'd never been with a girl for a straight hour and she just listened to him!!!

One time, while I was incarcerated in Beaumont, Texas, we were having "chicken on the bone" day in the lunchroom. Now this only comes around once a month, so it's a big day because those bones can be made into weapons. So, my homeboy, L, was being pressed to do stuff he didn't want to do. I remember he stuck that bone between his fingers with the sharp point sticking out. He walked up to this guy and hit him in the face with his lunch tray. When he did that, that bone popped this guy's eye right out. So see, prison is not a place you want to be.

Now I have a lot of stories about prison, but let me tell you the horrible reality. I was in a transition center for about a week. A couple doors down, I heard people sounding like they were wrestling at first. But then the wrestling stopped, and it turned to a man pleading and asking other men not to rape him. You hear this, and you hear this a lot, and you hear fights and stabbings, and you hear what it sounds like when a knife penetrates someone. You try to transition from this, but in reality, your mind and the way you think from that point on is fucked up. Ultimately, I don't think a person can ever really shake it.

Leonard Peltier was my cellmate in Florida. He is a Native American (mostly Ojibwe) activist who, after becoming one of the

best-known indigenous rights activists in North America, was convicted of murdering two Federal Bureau of Investigation (FBI) agents. Peltier belonged to the American Indian Movement (AIM), which sought to draw attention to federal violations of Native American treaty rights; he was found guilty of the killings in 1977 and has since been in federal prison, currently in Florida. To this day, he maintains that he was not the one responsible for killing the agents.

Peltier became a key member of the American Indian Movement. He worked to end police brutality, racism, and provide the community—especially elders—with assistance, food, and supplies. He also became a personal friend.

On June 27, 2014, I submitted a letter to the San Francisco Bay View newspaper. Here is the article:

Leonard Peltier, my cellmate: Simple man with a big vision

by Anthony Eagle

I would like to take this opportunity to give you positive praise. Your newspaper is absolutely wonderful. It shows the reality of society inside prison walls and also society outside these prison walls. I am currently being housed in federal prison, United States Penitentiary, or USP, Coleman 1 in Coleman, Florida. My cellmate is an inspiration to all ethnic groups who has endured the injustices by the hands of what we call the "government." His name is Leonard Peltier, in prison since 1975 for a crime he didn't commit. How can someone hate when all that's asked for is "peace and equality"? Am I asking too much? Are we asking too much? Let me tell you about myself. I am 29 years old. I am Indian from the Ojibwe People out of Michigan, currently doing time in federal prison for taking a stand against sex abuse, protecting my people for being a voice, a voice for the scared, timid, hurt and silent.

Our people have suffered the same way over the years. The pain is still visible today when we look in our communities and see alcoholism, drug addiction, poverty. In my way of life, we have a ceremony called a "sweat." This is a chance to suffer through hot rocks and physical pain. I cry for the shared pain we hold. I cry for the teens affected by  suicide. How did we get to that point? If I could carry you, I would.

My heart is in limbo daily by being behind these walls and seeing all these lost men searching for meaning. People, remember I said, "a simple man with a big vision." My vision is this: to write with all people of injustice not for the purpose of war but for peace, so we may start to heal. I ask you to stand with me. My time here is short – seven months till I am back fighting for you. By asking for peace and being productive, we will move mountains. In the Native way, we are called warriors, and also in your way of life. So please, no more crimes against the people or easy money. By doing this we give into the plan built against us. So, please, I offer my hand to yours, brothers and sisters, to join this way of life for the greater good of both our races, Blacks and Indians. Please write to me with your ideas and support.

Leonard was like a father figure, and he was so special to me. He gave me my back tattoo- AIM: American Indian Movement, and I smoked pot in the sweat lodge for the first time with Leonard, in the middle of the prison yard. We had to split up after beating up another group of inmates. But, Leonard held his own!!

You are not unique in prison. It's going to take time to learn, but prison is a place to learn a lesson. I realized I was growing as a person mentally. I was free, but the prison changed me because it helped me look into myself. I had to be the best version of myself, so I became the man I am now, and I appreciated life and family so much more.

I was about to go home for a third time, walking around the yard, everyone yelling at me that I was going to get to go out and party or find a girl to fuck, and it got so old, that's all they had to say to me. I've done some horrific things, and I knew what I had to get through to get here. In prison, you are just another body.

In this picture, I was locked up-arrested for my first felony home invasion. I got super sick, and no one helped me. They released me because I was sick and had to get radiation treatment – discovered I had a hyperthyroid. This picture is me and my dad. You can see how much weight I had lost because no one took the time to find out what was wrong. If it wasn't for my family, I would've just wasted away and died behind bars.

I guess if I could say anything good about being locked up, it helped me battle my inner demons and discover who I really needed to be as a man and father. Unfortunately, I had to learn my lessons the hard way. It's through my experiences that I am praying my kids don't repeat the generational cycle of incarceration. My dad wanted the same thing towards the end of his life, but it was already too late for him to have that positive impact on me. My life mirrors his, and now I am at the point where I can finally continue what he started.

ANTHONY EAGLE, JR.

7 GOOD WOLF, BAD WOLF

I ask for wisdom and strength, not to be superior to my brothers, but to be able to fight my greatest enemy, myself.

- Ojibwe prayer

Mine is a story of sadness, of being alone, and not knowing where to turn to when you have nobody. But in the same story, it's a story of triumph, where I become victorious in myself, and start believing in myself.

See prison can be viewed many different ways. A person can say prison is this or that when they come out, but let's get one thing straight, what prison really is, is LONELY. It's not a place you want to be, but prison changed my life for the good.

I really started thinking about what I put out into the world. I wondered why it was so hard to love another human being unconditionally. Why is it so hard to reciprocate the love of God in that way? I mean, eventually, you start to put these conditions on your partner because you see something you don't like, and you never really just love that person for who they are. Why do we keep doing that? Why can't WE change?

I had so much time to just sit and think. Who am I? Who do I want to be? What did my choices do to my kids? Will I ever be able to earn back their trust and respect? Not a day went by while I was locked up that I didn't think about them. Now that I was finally out, I made the decision to change myself, my way of thinking, my entire mindset, so that I wouldn't end up in prison ever again. I had to be here for my kids.

Read this story about the two wolves within us all, and maybe you'll understand what we all struggle with on a daily basis.

One evening, an elderly Cherokee brave told his grandson about a battle that goes on inside all people.
He said, "My son, the battle is between two wolves inside us all.
One wolf is evil.
It is anger, envy, jealousy, sorrow, regret, greed, arrogance, self-pity, guilt, resentment, inferiority, lies, false pride, superiority, defeat, and ego.
The other wolf is good.
It is joy, peace, love, hope, serenity, humility, kindness, benevolence, empathy, generosity, effort, truth, compassion, and faith."
The grandson thought about it for a minute and then asked his grandfather:
"Which wolf wins?"
The old Cherokee simply replied, "The one you feed."

This story has so much wisdom and has helped guide me along this journey. The struggle is beautiful. Without the struggle, I would not have grown into the man I am becoming. Struggles help us realize that we can persevere. They mold us, crushing us under the pressure so we come out bolder and chiseled. Struggles also force us to reach out to our highest source of strength.

When I got out, I was stuck in a halfway house. I had my own apartment there until my probation officer told me I had to get out to make room for someone else. I decided to get back with my ex, got kicked out and ended up homeless with my boys. We went to a hotel and that's when I decided to do my first TikTok.

I questioned how in the world I ended up homeless. Bad choices, and not doing something different was my downfall. I called the kid's grandma (on their mother's side) and we stayed with her two days. I was searching for jobs and finally got hired as a welder in Iron Mountain, Michigan and got a house for me and my boys. I earned a welding certificate in prison and utilized it so I knew I would always find a job.

I will always struggle. That's just a fact of life. I deal with depression, PTSD, anger, and addictions. Sometimes the bad wolf comes out roaring and gnashing inside my brain and I feel myself giving in to it's cries. When I tell you that my kids are my saving grace, please believe me. If I had to fight these demons all alone, I'm not sure I would make it out of here. My kids encourage the good wolf inside of me. I have to stay strong so that the good wolf will win.

I've made horrible choices. I spent years and years away from my kids to fix my wrongs. Not a day went by that my heart didn't long to see the smiles on my son's and daughter's faces. I'll spend the rest of my life trying to make it up to them and praying that they don't go down the same paths that I chose.

Sometimes life still gets to me. When the rules change, the monster inside of me wants to come out and scream. I fight this daily. To keep myself under control, to battle my fears with a clear head and not be clouded by things I keep buried inside. The will to change is strong, but I'd be lying if I said it was easy. It's not easy... but it's worth it in the end.

ANTHONY EAGLE, JR.

8 I'LL MAKE YA' FAMOUS

And be a simple kind of man, Oh be something you love and
understand, Baby be a simple kind of man, Oh won't you do
this for me son, if you can.

-Lynyrd Skynyrd

ANTHONY EAGLE, JR.

When I stumbled upon TikTok, I wasn't searching to become known. I just needed something to help me get out of my depression and watching other people's videos helped me. So, I decided to jump in and try to post some motivating videos and share a glimpse of my life and my story. I had no idea it would resonate with so many people. So, in a way, all of you were a huge part of my pushing through mental obstacles, going from being homeless to becoming a homeowner, from being alone to now being part of a loving family. So, for that, I will always be thankful for YOU!

In the same way, I didn't start out looking for love. I mean, yeah, I definitely met my share of women, but while the idea of finding love is great, I also felt like it was something that may never happen for me again. I'm a broken human being, and that brokenness runs a lot of people off. They want me to be this idea that they have in their mind but when it comes to the real-life shit, unconditional love hasn't existed for me.

Kat and I met after Ella started watching signing videos. Kat had taught her some signs when she was a baby, so she would watch videos on TikTok. Ella kept encouraging Kat to send me a message and I briefly replied a few times.

Then, we FaceTimed and we wanted to meet each other but were both scared, scared of how we were feeling because we knew it was intense, but when we made the decision to meet I got cold feet. We both thought it was crazy because we barely knew each other, but Kat asked me if I wanted her to come to me, and I said yes, so I switched the flight for her.

Kat spent five days with me, and we both knew it was love. When she left, I was going to come visit her, but then we decided we didn't want to separate again and, as crazy as it sounds, I moved 1020 miles to take a chance on love. It's changed everyone's lives in a way that neither one of us ever could imagine. Two broken people breaking the cycle of everything that we've both endured. Our families thought we were crazy, but neither one of us wanted to ever have a regret...

Love has always been an emotionally charged, passionate, and chaotic experience. I thrive on the excitement and euphoric feelings. But self-sabotage comes into play when things begin settling and life becomes "normal" and routine. I allow my boredom, or what I perceive as boredom, to convince me that there must be something wrong, that I need to go, move, find something else to make me excited. I'm a gypsy at heart, I hate being stagnant, but I also hold a fear that if I allow myself to love and be loved, inevitably something bad will happen and I'll just end up being hurt. I had to be broken in order to finally love myself. And, in loving myself, I am finally able to love someone else.

I started sharing my knowledge of native hand talk online by signing to music and posting the videos. It made me proud to be able to show people that part of my culture, to share something that many people had no idea of. But in doing so, I also received a ton of backlash from the deaf community who thought that I was trying to gain popularity and profit through ASL- American Sign Language.

I had to speak up for myself and educate everyone about the history of native hand talk, but many still did not want to accept the fact that I wasn't treading over them. I actually do not use ASL, I use a combination of hand talk and SEE- signing exact English. I am a constant learner and strive each day to become more fluent in signing.

Could you imagine not being able to communicate except for with your hands? Wouldn't it be better if the world understood how to communicate with you and understood your point of view? My intentions were pure. I just didn't expect some of the things that were thrown at me. But, like everything else, I just persevered and refused to back down. In doing so, I was able to get with other creators who were also being bullied and give them the strength to stand up for themselves and their passion for signing.

I started gaining more followers and developed my own anthem once I started signing to the song Welcome to My House by Nu Breed and Jesse Howard. People really gravitated to my video when I played this song and I hit my first million views. Since then, I make a point of signing to that song whenever I'm in a new area or state. My first time on stage was with the band. They let me come up and sign while they played the song. What a rush! That pretty much solidified my passion for performing.

Things were going great, I was gaining more followers every day and reaching a larger audience. Then, the unthinkable happened. We were moving to a new house. I was getting the refrigerator ready to put on the truck and it fell back, crushing my hand against the wall. It wasn't the pain, I can handle that, it was the mental fright of going through another surgery and wondering what I was going to do because, up to that point, people were following me to watch me sign. How would I continue to sign with one good hand? My amazing followers were able to help me raise over $3000 to go towards the cost of my surgery. My hand healed nicely, and I was able to use it again with minimal issues. I'm so thankful for all of you.

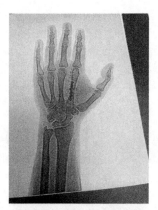
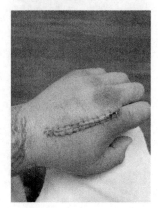

Now, my goal is to spread love, motivate, and encourage everyone to live life sharing joy and positive energy. I'm still human, but I fully believe that we are made of energy and exist to vibrate at a higher energy level and share that energy with one another. I cannot wait to start visiting with everyone at book signings and speaking engagements. You have truly fueled my passion to help and inspire others.

ANTHONY EAGLE, JR.

9. CREATING A NEW GENERATION

It's up to us to break generational curses. When they say, 'It runs in the
family,' you tell them, 'This is where it runs out.'"
                                                                    -Tiny Buddha

My value isn't based on things. True value comes in the form of happiness and spreading love. I want to inspire people to be the best they can be. The things you go through on a daily basis is hard and not meant for everyone to experience. Some of us go through extra shit and it's meant to tell us what we're worth.

Every day I see people living in fear, wrapped up in their comfortable living and security. The only thing real in life is the relationships you are building. You can get lost in the material things and the daily schedule, but they only take you away from what is really important.

It's crucial that you find your voice. Question things that don't match your worth. No one is better than anyone else, but your self-worth is worth millions.

Give yourself permission to be free to build confidence and boost your morale. When are you going to do that for yourself? It's okay to turn it around. We all have bad days. But we all must find the beauty in the bad moment, in what comes and what's revealed to you is the most beautiful thing in the world. Learning to look at life from that perspective all the time, oh my gosh, you don't just live life- you enjoy life! And I'd rather have the shortest life ever enjoying it, then the longest life not living

If you battle an addiction and you relapse, and let's say you had a lot of time in, it's not about the years, stop getting so caught up in the years. The moment you grew is the moment you relapsed and realized you needed to do something about it. Now it's time to change, that's the growth, that's the lesson. Sober time is good to set as a goal, but its only about what you are learning.

No matter what you do, don't give up, keep putting one foot in front of the other and those bad days will turn to good days, and them bad days become distant memories and hopefully become forgotten. But right now, you are the game changer, so starting now set goals, move forward, have an opinion, make it count and keep loving.

My goal is to establish a place on reservations to teach this new generation a trade, to teach them how to establish independence and wealth for their family. I want to empower them so that they will have other options besides just relying on the government to provide for them. There is a poverty mindset that has been passed down from generation to generation. It's time to rewrite that script!!

YRB- Young Red and Beautiful is going to be a schooling program to help aid and assist Native American children to advance in society through entrepreneurship. They will learn the skills necessary to professionally run and operate their own business.

This will be a three-year program with it's own curriculum and trainers. The first year will be designed around academic work, bookwork, learning government contracts, trading, learning about government laws pertaining to business, and state laws pertaining to business.

The second year will focus on learning skills and trades necessary to improve their lives and their communities, and ultimately self reliance.

The third year will be establishing financial knowledge, the right mindset, and researching and obtaining grants and funding to create their own businesses.

Once they graduate the program, they will be required to give back to the community and the program by becoming part of the team that teaches the next group. Therefore, it is fully sustainable and regenerates with each new graduating class.

This program is to help strengthen the Native American population by enforcing the backbone and teaching our children how to own their own life, how to be the boss of what happens the next day, and most of all how to protect themselves from generational curses. This program is not going to hurt anybody. In fact, this program will succeed in limiting and ultimately destroying a lot of crimes that happen on the reservations that are simply nonsense. One day YRB is going to be in every tribe throughout the Americas and I cannot wait to hear about the success stories and the pride that will be instilled in these families.

10 WEAR IT LIKE ARMOUR

Therefore, put on the full armour of God, so that when the day of evil comes, you may be able to stand your ground, and after you have done everything, to stand.

-Ephesians 6:13 NIV

Heaven is real. God is real.

I'm telling you that as an absolute truth because in 2017 I died. I broke my ankle playing with my kids. We were flying a drone at a skate park – the drone got stuck on a half-pipe and I went to get it. My foot went under me, and it snapped. I had to have surgery immediately. It busted my tibia in half, so I needed a plate. The second surgery was to take the plate out because my body was rejecting it and I developed MRSA. After a third surgery, they sent me home. The screws snapped off and I was scheduled for a fourth surgery. I had to have a pic line and the surgery to clean it out. The pic line became infected, and MRSA got into my blood system. The cold you feel with an infection like that is indescribable. It was bone chilling. I had a pic line at my house, and when the medicine was put in, it sent me into septic shock. I passed out on the way to the hospital.

I saw a trail in the middle of the woods but the only trees there were huge red pines. The tops extended into the white light. It's like we were on this floating piece of land in the middle of this light. When you're on this light, it didn't matter if I walked backwards or forwards it still leads to the light. You don't realize it's not just light, when you walk into the light you feel peace, like a hug of love and peace. It blows away any concept of love you could ever realize. It was so beautiful, and you don't think of anything bad at all. You don't think of anything that was left behind.

When you walk into the light, things are revealed – rainbows with the craziest colors and water running through them. It was mystical, everywhere energy, surrounding you. I went towards the part where my dad was standing in front of me in the light. He didn't say a word, we just communicated with our minds. He told me everything was all right and there would not be any more hurt, just to come home to the light. I told him I couldn't stay there because I had to go back and take care of my kids.

Suddenly I woke up in the emergency room. They had pronounced me dead, and the doctors were walking away. My wife at the time was trying to get in and I yelled out just let her in. The doctors were tripping!! They turned around quickly and went to me. The next I know I was in ICU for eight days.

The experience affected what I believe. It put me at peace of heart and peace of mind here because I know where I'm going.
My pain was my motivation, and my children became my strength. My heart becomes stronger and heals every single day. In this life, we have a purpose, a plan for good. How can we impact lives? Society would have us to believe that men don't suffer emotionally, but the reality is it's okay to not be okay, and it's okay to seek help.

Half the people that sought to destroy me and my name could never get through the miles I put on these feet.

I've had many relationships, many marriages, and I'm still on this journey of self-discovery. I know what it means to love and be loved, but I also know what it feels like to be heartbroken and thought of as a burden. Love comes with a price, and there's always a risk of failure. But I'd rather love many times then never know what it feels like to have that love reciprocated. Give your heart to any kind of relationship and watch it grow.

The struggle is beautiful. Without the struggle, I would not have grown into the man I am becoming. Struggles help us realize that we can persevere. They mold us, crushing us under the pressure so we come out bolder and chiseled. Struggles also force us to reach out to our highest source of strength.

How do you get motivated to change the world? You realize you can't. At some point you must realize that you can only change yourself, and in doing so you touch others. It's a beautiful thing when love is spread through joy and kindness.

It's not the hardships and the heartaches that made me who I am, it's the compassion after those heartaches that made me who I am. When I showed love and compassion to those that others didn't think deserved it, that is what made me who I am today because at one point tomorrow was never promised to me either. At one point, I was no longer on this earth, but I was shown the deepest love, and I was shown how to love YOU, a perfect stranger. So, I tell you, love more and be THAT person.

Life can feel so complicated, so overwhelming. It can break the strongest person down and send ripple effects into the lives of people they love the most. I understand this so well because I have been living in the nightmare for the past few years. The reality of who I was in the worst ways helped me learn who I was in the best way.

The struggles that I have went through broke me apart, but in the end sparked a fire to always be the better part of me. Out of all my years thinking I had life by the horns, I was living in fear, shame, and guilt. Allowing my own thoughts to control my actions.

I was afraid of failure. Guess what I failed? I failed my children, my family, my friends, and myself by making the choices that led me to prison. By making the choice to give into my drug addiction. All these choices kept me fueled by shame, guilt, remorse, loneliness, and fear.

Refusing to recognize who I was in my worst didn't allow me to grow. It did the opposite. It enslaved me, held me hostage because fear made me believe that I had to hide the scary parts of Anthony because nobody will understand. They will only judge me or make fun of me.

Prison can be many things. I promise what you think prison is, it's not. For me, prison became my liberator by allowing me to slow down and deal with life on a sober level. I finally can see clearly, and the funniest thing happened. All of my fears that held me down became the very thing that set me free.

I didn't like my fears and acted like they never happened. Instead, I now wear them because they are a part of who I am. "My story". I am an ex-con that spent years in prison. I am a drug addict that struggles daily but wins with each day sober. I did fail my children and my loved ones as a friend, father, and brother, but now I have each day to redeem myself and be the best version of me for them.

All of these things held me down in the bowels of depression, that have sparked thoughts of suicide, became my armour. Why? Because the very ugly truth is that I was only this because I didn't want to see past what I would hide from society, friends, and family only because they would use this to hurt me, which was only my own fear. I broke that fear, embraced what I had done, acknowledged how I was spreading hurt into the very places I would say I loved and installing pollution into the city I called home. Which I am so very sorry for all of this.

I wear my fears like armour because each day I share my story of hope this no longer becomes my personal prison. I grow a little bit each time into the "Man" I always knew I was but had no clue how I was going to reach it. By exposing those truths, they lose their accent of fear. And as they say the weight has been lifted.

I share my story with all of you as a beacon of hope that there is a way, but also in hopes that you will be bold and share your story. I do this most of all for me. Like I said each time I relive the ugly, it loses its grip of fear. So, in the end I hope you help yourself because each day I heal mine. Reach inside and look at all of the love that is behind you and love yourself for the sober days and thank God for the release!!

I strive each day to show love and spread joy, even as I battle inner demons. We all have good and evil inside of us.

After all, the devil was an angel, too.

ANTHONY EAGLE, JR.

ABOUT THE AUTHOR

We all have a choice to be the good wolf or the bad wolf.
We all have a choice to be an angel or a devil.
Some of us choose to walk the path of the devil or choose to walk
the Godly path.
Just remember, the devil was an angel, too.

Anthony Eagle, Jr., better known as Chrimsan to his followers, is from the Ojibwe tribe in Michigan. His life started out with the innocence and curiosity of a child, and quickly turned in another direction. For many years, he lived a hard and dangerous life, with a couple of terms spent in prison. At the end of his last prison sentence, he became determined to do better and become the father that his children needed.

My dad's book was the beginning.

My book continues the story.

My sister's book will be the final chapter.

To be continued….

MENTAL HEALTH RESOURCES

People often don't get the mental help they need because they don't know where to start.

Talk to your primary care doctor or another health professional about mental health problems. Ask them to connect you with the right mental health services.

If you do not have a health professional who is able to assist you, use these resources to find help for yourself, your friends, your family, or your students.

Emergency Medical Services- 911

If the situation is potentially life-threatening, get immediate emergency assistance by calling 911, available 24 hours a day.

Suicide & Crisis Lifeline – CALL 988

If you or someone you know is suicidal or in emotional distress, contact the 988 Suicide & Crisis Lifeline. Trained crisis workers are available to talk 24 hours a day, 7 days a week. Your confidential and toll-free call goes to the nearest crisis center in the Lifeline national network.

These centers provide crisis counseling and mental health referrals.

Call or text   988 or chat   988lifeline.org.

National Hotline for Substance Abuse and Mental Health:

1-866-903-3787

Find Treatment with SAMHSA

SAMHSA's <u>Behavioral Health Treatment Services Locator</u> is a confidential and anonymous source of information for persons seeking treatment facilities in the United States or U.S. Territories for substance use/addiction and/or mental health problems.

https://findtreatment.samhsa.gov/

If you are currently incarcerated or an ex-prisoner, there are federal and state resources to help you.

https://www.justice.gov/archive/fbci/progmenu_programs.html

ANTHONY EAGLE, JR.

Printed in Great Britain
by Amazon

19634924R00059